Steve Waltman is a native of Bedford, Pa, and now resides in Pittsburgh with his wife, Jackie. He retired in 2017 as a guidance counselor at Bedford High School, where Waltman also served as the Boys Varsity Basketball coach for eight seasons. Steve and Jackie have three sons and eleven grandchildren. His writing history includes two stories on Kindle e-book, two years as a contributor to Robert Makinson's Comedy Service (Brooklyn, NY), and selling stand-up comedy to Joan Rivers. His most recent work, *Some Things I Think I Said* was published in 2022 by Austin Macauley Publishers.

To William "Lemon" Bradford, my protagonist, the straw that stirs the drink and my friend. I thank him for including me in his personal quest and allowing me to write about it.

Steve Waltman

HOW LEMON HAPPENED – BELTZHOOVER PRIDE

AUSTIN MACAULEY PUBLISHERS™

LONDON • CAMBRIDGE • NEW YORK • SHARJAH

Ordering Information
Quantity sales: Special discounts are available on quantity purchases by corporations, associations, and others. For details, contact the publisher at the address below.

Publisher's Cataloging-in-Publication data
Waltman, Steve
How Lemon Happened – Beltzhoover Pride

ISBN 9798891553057 (Paperback)
ISBN 9798891553064 (ePub e-book)

Library of Congress Control Number: 2024902453

www.austinmacauley.com/us

First Published 2024
Austin Macauley Publishers LLC
40 Wall Street, 33rd Floor, Suite 3302
New York, NY 10005
USA

mail-usa@austinmacauley.com
+1 (646) 5125767

I need to thank the following contributors to this story. Their ability to share their hearts and memories made this book possible – Malcolm Williams, Mabel Bradford Washington, Gary Washington, Helen Bradford Roberts, George Bradford, Dot Bradford Reese, William "Lemon" Bradford, Steven McCray, Carrie McCray, Lynn McCray Kingdom, Janice Tyler, Gloria, Joyce, Sharon Johnson, Karen Johnson.

Lemon leaned back in his chair and cocked his head. "Stephen, I'm telling you, you've got to write a second one." I noticed Lemon had switched from calling me Steeeve to Stephen. No big deal, but I wondered why. Maybe he didn't like the way it looked in the first story. Maybe he thought it made him look slow. It didn't matter enough to ask him about it.

"Christ Lemon, we'd be lucky if fifty people read When Lemon Happened. It's not like the country is demanding a sequel!" I just figured he wanted to see his name in print again.

"Stephen, you don't understand! The first one was through your eyes, those two years in Bedford. But you don't know what led up to all that. You don't know what happened. That's why you've got to do it, I'm telling you! I gotta take you to Beltzhoover so you can see!"

Damn Lemon, always poking and prodding me to write, like I'm John Updike. He was starting to annoy me. Lemon was a literary pyromaniac. I'll be damned if it didn't work. "Okay," I said. "I will at least think about it, see where it all began." Lemon broke into a wide grin. He sensed victory.

"Man, Stephen, you've got to go! And it's got to be no bullshit, just like John Waltman!"

Referencing the intensity of my late father, I thought he must really be desperate. He then asked me how I would write and what I would want it to mean. Again, the literary pyromaniac striking the match.

I assured Lemon that it would be no bullshit if I did it. "I don't know, haven't even thought about it. Not sure I can do it." (I knew I'd be doing it.) "But, If I do, this one has to be bigger than us."

It seemed almost every time I met Lemon in the past six years, he was either getting over a surgery or about to get another one. Apparently, the original surgery for prostate cancer had damaged his urethra. Three surgeries later, the problem persisted. His last one was so disastrous that he was life-flighted to Pittsburgh for emergency surgery. Afterwards, the surgeon informed him that he very easily could have died. Another surgery would be scheduled in July, this time in Pittsburgh, to finally correct the issue once and for all.

Lemon, now 67, and I, 65, had traveled quite a distance from the basketball courts of our youth.

No more running and dunking for Lemon; the hard drives and deep shots long gone for me. Basketball is, after all, a young man's game. With Lemon, though, I could still see traces of the athlete he once was, while he maintained the outgoing personality of his youth. For me, I'm not sure. It is always more difficult to evaluate yourself. Although, still lean at 6'0" 180, I have to wonder how others view me. But all of that is more curiosity than concern. When you get older, sometimes you just don't give a shit. However, Lemon, and blacks in general, must worry about how they are perceived. A traffic violation or a peaceful protest are events that white people don't break a sweat over. For blacks, they can be life-threatening.

After our long lunch, in an odd twist, Lemon headed home to Bedford while I hit the turnpike to Pittsburgh. Two weeks after retiring, my wife, Jackie, and I moved to Pittsburgh to be near five of our grandchildren. Lemon had temporarily moved back to Bedford. near his sister Mable and her husband. Gary 'Goo' Washington, whom I will discuss later. His stay is looking a bit more permanent now that he's been there for two years. Lemon has a love-hate affair with my hometown of Bedford. He had an overall positive experience in his two years at Bedford High School. A talented athlete and artist with a gregarious personality, Lemon was largely well-received by his white classmates. Had he been a tuba player in the marching band, perhaps the outcome would have been different. Bedford, like many communities across the country, places a huge emphasis on sports. Without a doubt, that worked to his benefit.

Yet Lemon, in the 70s and today, can't escape the vibe that Bedford is an uptight, conservative, closet-racist place. The plethora of Trump signs throughout the area made him uneasy as well. A return to Pittsburgh could certainly be in his future once his health issues stabilize.

On the two-hour drive home, I thought more about the perceptions of Lemon and me by white America. I know the way I am viewed is probably much more favorable than the perceptions Lemon would elicit. It is wrong and hurtful, but it is still a reality today. Navigating the turns and elevation of the turnpike, my mind took me to just how much I have appropriated from black culture at no price. Earl 'The

Pearl's' spin dribble, Walt Frazier's behind the back, I took and made mine. Motown and Soul Train allowed me a peek into black feeling and soul but without the challenges and pain of being African American. Hell, even in Little League I was making basket catches a la Willie Mays and Roberto Clemente. It was precisely these kinds of thoughts that began to make me eager to write the second one. I just needed that spark, that damn literary firebug, Lemon! Oh yeah, I thought, this one was definitely going to be bigger.

During the last six years, our conversations always came back to the first story, with the possibility of a second one lingering in the air like a mix of Glade and bad gas. When Lemon Happened encouraged him to examine his life in totality. Now, looking at his family and its past, he was trying to put the pieces together to figure it all out. It's why he keeps pushing for the second one. He wants more help, more clarity in his search for meaning.

Looking back on it, as a young small-town teen, Lemon was more of a cartoon superhero than a real person. I didn't really know him; how could I have? Lemon didn't know me as well. Yet we were open to each other, which has carried over all these many years. Friends, yes, but much different than the ones I grew up with. My Bedford buddies, though I rarely see them, have always been a constant in my life. Whereas Lemon has popped in and out of my life, at times more of a loose thought than a solid person. I wonder if, even for him, it might feel that way. Who was he? Who is he? I don't think he knows. He's counting on that second story.

Driving through the Squirrel Hill Tunnel, I thought this next one would have to be bigger and deeper. How Lemon Happened will be more of an excavation than a story.

I had never seen Lemon appear so focused. He wheeled into my driveway in the North Hills of Pittsburgh with a wide grin on his face. He popped out of his car with a briefcase in his hand and said, "You ready?"

Slightly perturbed, I replied, "Yeah, for the past 45 minutes. Thought we were meeting Malcolm at 11:30." It was almost 12:30.

Lemon paid no attention to my irritation. "Didn't start as soon. Had to get gas, then a breakfast sandwich. Traffic was bad, Stephen!" I nodded, holding my legal pad. "Okay, let's go."

"Hop in, my brother, we're going to Eat n Park!" I cleared a bag of chips off the passenger seat and jumped in.

The hostess led us to a table near the back. A handsome, broad-shouldered black man was sitting with a skeptical, disgusted sideways stare directed toward Lemon. Lemon quickly introduced us, then gave Malcom the identical explanation for being an hour tardy. Malcolm seemed disinterested, then asked us if we were having lunch. Apparently moving onto dessert, Malcom ordered apple pie a la mode. Since I had lunch too, waiting for Lemon, I went for the same as Malcolm. Lemon ordered tacos.

Malcolm is Lemon's older half-brother, same mother, a different father. Over ten years older than Lemon, he often wasn't around for Lemon's 'wonder years' Asked what he most remembered about Lemon as a youngster, Malcolm, with his serious countenance, offered that Lemon, being the baby of the family, was spoiled. Lemon, sitting next to

Malcolm in the booth, leaned back away from him with an expression of disbelief.

Malcolm, annoyed with Lemon's theatrics, told me stone-faced that Lemon was the only member of the family not to take a beating from Mr. Bradford (his dad). His only other appraisal of his younger brother was that his "heart was too big." Malcolm claimed that Lemon always allowed girls to rule him. Lemon shook his head in disagreement, but Malcom came back with, "Man, you know that's true!"

Not very verbose, I wasn't sure if Malcom didn't trust me or if he was still angry at Lemon for his late arrival. The retired city sanitation worker, looking as fit as a much younger man, became more animated when he moved the subject of discussion away from Lemon. Some big 'Q' talk took hold, and Malcom wondered if I was aware of what was in store within the next couple of months. JFK Jr. was still alive and would be showing up shortly. That, I said, was unbeknownst to me. Also, the ex-President would take over the reins again in August. That same month, Elvis and Michael Jackson would reappear because they had never died. While Lemon rolled his eyes in disgust, I simply said to Malcolm, "August is going to be one hell of a month!"

Since Malcolm didn't have much to say about Lemon's childhood, we wrapped the conversation up, and Malcom kindly paid the bill. We shook hands and were soon on our way to the scene of the crimes, Beltzhoover.

Green Tree to Beltzhoover isn't much over ten minutes, but like most cities, it is more than enough time to enter you into a different world. Lemon's relaxed, casual driving didn't necessarily put me at ease. He spent too much time glancing at me while we talked than on the road. "Watch it," I said more than once.

"Stephen, this is my area; I'm good!" Taking a left off 51, we climbed a steep ladder until we reached a sign that pointed Mt. Oliver right and Beltzhoover left. We went left, while the whole trip up from 51, we were next to McKinley Park, a nice area that stood in stark contrast to the beaten-down streets of Beltzhoover that we were approaching. Lemon mentioned it was this park where both he and his older brother George would run and workout in preparation for their athletics. Near the top of McKinley Park sat a nice-looking basketball court with glass backboards. They had resurfaced the court and painted it. Beyond the baseline were the large painted words BELTZHOOVER PRIDE.

"Looks better now," Lemon said. "Man, the court was rough back in the day. We'd play all year, even in the cold. Even after regular practice, we'd come and work on dunks." Lemon laughed.

"I'm telling you, Stephen, it would be dark! But it was the style of the dunk that mattered. We all tried to outdo each other. Man, Stephen!" Lemon flashed that wide grin while shaking his head and not paying much attention to the road.

As Lemon eased into Beltzhoover, he looked at me with that big grin and said, "You'll be the only white today, my brother!"

"Hey, not the first time for me." Lemon appeared doubtful. "When else?"

I told him the story of spending most of my Summer of 1979 at Slippery Rock University, finishing my coursework before starting my student teaching in the fall. I had my classes in the morning, then would head to the field house and play basketball in the afternoon. I had myself back in playing shape. It was the most ball I'd played since that lost senior year of manic depression. My shot was back, and the quick first step to the hole had returned. A summer league of six teams had been developed, and I was playing in one of them. We did pretty well and found ourselves in the championship game against an all-black team, which featured a couple of players from Slippery Rock's team. It was a decent game, but they were better and won by at least 15 points.

Their team had two gorgeous black girls come to all their games. They showed up again for that title game in the fieldhouse. Always standing behind the one basket on the second level where the track was, they would voice their approval or displeasure during the game. I noticed they called out my name a few times and waved. I figured they were toying with me or simply trying to distract me from the game. I didn't mind either way; I was simply pleased they knew my name. From way back in the 70s until now, I have considered black women, in general, to be the most appealing of all. Although happily married for 37 years to my attractive, white wife, it's been black women who seem to most grab my attention. Beyond looks, they possess a sensuality, spirituality, and strength that is unique.

After the loss in that title game, a couple of players from the champions approached me and asked if I would join their team for a summer league in New Castle, a small city just west of Slippery Rock. Feeling in the groove, I gladly accepted. A few days later, we took a van to New Castle on a hot July evening. As we approached the outdoor court with a high chain-linked fence around it, it quickly became clear we were in an all-black section, and I was the only white person around. My brand-new teammates, all black, began to howl. Between their loud laughter, one said, "Steve! You're the only European!" They got a real kick out of that. It was a bit startling to be the only white man in a crowd of players, fans, and 'referees'. 'Referees', because in the game before us, although both had whistles dangling from their necks, they were used sparingly. Instead, most of their attention was paid to the beers in their hands and the joints between their lips. During our game, I felt the fans strongly against us and had the same feeling about the refs. It was rough and physical, but we rarely went to the foul line. Being out-of-towners seemed to work against us, and perhaps they didn't appreciate me being there. We dropped a close one, and we immediately got out of town. My black teammates were truly disgusted by the beating we took and vowed not to return. I was actually okay with that.

Lemon had us on a tight schedule. Next on the agenda was Steve 'Chub' McCray, an old neighbor and friend from Lemon's youth. "He'll be good, Stephen." Lemon seemed sure. We drove up another steep grade, then turned into a dirt alley, which led us to the back of Carrie McCray's house. Chub was outside on this warm June afternoon doing some yard work. He paused and looked as Lemon pulled up. Once Lemon stepped out of his car, Chub smiled and slowly walked toward us. Short and stocky, Steve McCray seemed to have a calm and easy manner about him as he greeted his old friend and met me.

He led us into the house, where I met his mother, Carrie, a sweet-looking woman probably close to my mother's age.

I immediately noticed a spark in her eyes, like she was still interested in everything and wouldn't miss anything. Also at the kitchen table was Chub's sister Lynn, who was an attractive lady probably close in age to her brother. Both Mrs. McCray and Lynn were pleased to see Lemon and gave him warm hugs. Lemon sat down with them while Steve offered me a bottle of water and led me to the outside deck. There seemed to be no confusion about why I was there, and Chub was more than ready to give me a history lesson.

Chub was professorial in his delivery. Soft-spoken and deliberate, he started me off with some background history of Beltzhoover itself. The name Beltzhoover came from a German farmer who once owned all the land that became Beltzhoover. I figured land so steep and high wasn't appealing to a farmer, or perhaps caused him vertigo.

Growing up in Beltzhoover was much different in the late 50s to early 70s, than it is today, Chub was quick to point out. Now, Beltzhoover is occasionally featured on Pittsburgh news for shootings and arson. Then, it was bustling with activity and enterprise, and the community was tight-knit. In its heyday, Beltzhoover boasted a dozen or more mom-and-pop stores, had three physicians, several dry cleaners, four bars, an A&P and a movie theater. It was a self-contained neighborhood, so it wasn't necessary to frequent downtown Pittsburgh. A 'small Tulsa' ran through my head. I wondered what ended Beltzhoover's run of prosperity. Another government attack?

Surprisingly, Steve said that nearly half the population was white throughout the 60s. There was a neighborhood elementary and junior high school within walking distance.

It was a close community where everyone seemed to look after one another. Two parents were the norm, and often both worked. The steel mills and post offices were major employers, along with the various businesses that lined the streets of Beltzhoover.

A couple of events literally changed the complexion of Beltzhoover. When steel mills slowed down and eventually closed, it had a drastic effect on all the people of Pittsburgh, including Beltzhoover. Also, the building of the Civic Arena in the lower Hill District displaced many black families and forced them to crowd into the upper Hill district or move to areas like Beltzhoover. The influx of blacks made enough whites uncomfortable enough to leave as part of the 'white flight'. Over the course of several years, Beltzhoover went from a thriving area of Pittsburgh to an area with a much bleaker outlook.

Chub made a seamless transition from community discussion to himself and the McCray family.

Soon I discovered that Steve and I shared more than a first name. We both graduated from Slippery Rock State College, as it was known then. Unlike me, Steve had a desire to go into medicine in college. But early on at The Rock, he soon discovered he wasn't prepared for the rigor of pre-med science courses. He knew that South Hills High, a Pittsburgh public school, didn't have him up to speed with his classmates. Quickly, he became a business major.

During his college years, McCray played saxophone in a band that traveled to venues like Clarion and California Universities. Chub, accomplished at both alto sax and clarinet, was the first chair in the city. The music gigs provided him some extra spending money, and when probed, Chub acknowledged it wasn't a bad way to meet girls.

Tragedy met Steve McCray and his family in the mid-90s when, after giving birth to their daughter, his wife Connie had an aneurysm and passed away. It forced Steve and his other children to move in with his parents so they could help while he continued to work. Chub talked about those dark days in his measured, deliberate voice. He has stayed at his parents' home ever since.

Chub smiled at some of his earlier days in Beltzhoover when the McCrays lived across from Lemon and the rest of the Bradfords. This geography demonstrated that you didn't need ten minutes to travel to a different world; you could just cross the street. Chub recalled Lemon being a fun, active, and athletic kid. Each street in the neighborhood had so many kids close in age that they could form their own teams and compete against each other. The summers featured constant activity. Foot races, baseball, and basketball would have the youngsters fired up. Each street had its pride, and competition was fierce. They all loved it, and Chub added that it was great having Lemon on his side.

With so much youth running around, he noted that community parenting was almost a necessity. The close-knit neighbors kept an eye out for each other. Chub mentioned it was far from the case these days. Crime in Beltzhoover is much more common these days and much more accessible. The lack of jobs and the breakdown of the family are certainly major factors. We talked about the differences in white and black communities for some time. Chub, with a mix of amusement and disgust, spoke about how differently drug issues were handled. If you were addicted to heroin in a city, it was a crime. You did jail time. When heroin spread to white suburbia, it became a medical crisis. Instead of being jailed, whites were sent to rehab. It is also ironic that while many blacks still languish in prison for marijuana crimes, it is legal in many states. Welcome to criminal justice in America!

Injustice at South Hills High School in the 60s and 70s hadn't escaped Steve McCray either. Chub said football coaches would actively promote white players and send out films to colleges, but black stars didn't get quite the attention. His own sister, Lynn, was also a victim of injustice in high school. Lynn McCray, an attractive and athletic girl, made South Hills High School history by becoming the first black girl to make the gymnastics team. When a television station came to interview the successful team, every gymnast was notified except Lynn. She missed the interview and a chance to appear on TV. Despite that slight, Lynn went on to become a college graduate and a high school Spanish teacher for years in Florida and Texas. She returned home in recent years to help with her mother after a significant illness.

Although acutely aware of these inequalities that remain in society, McCray didn't come across as bitter. In fact, far from it. He said he was brought up not to look for excuses. You know the lay of the land, and you make the most of it. Working hard and staying positive are the best methods for a path to happiness. Chub McCray, 'The Professor', was impressing the hell out of me.

He stated that perhaps on another visit it would be wise to speak with his mother, Carrie. She had been a staple of the community and could speak to the history of

Beltzhoover. Totally involved in their lives, his mom would routinely attend school board meetings, so she was always aware. Chub, also with a sense of pride, talked about his mom being a cafeteria worker who was known for 'the wave'. So in tune with the students, Mrs. McCray would wave the students through the line who couldn't afford to pay before the days of free and reduced lunches.

During our cafeteria discussion, Lemon made his way out onto the deck. "Man, it's been an hour and a half!" Lemon sounded astonished. "Stephen on Stephen, one-on-one, Ha!"

Lemon remained standing and nodded his head toward the kitchen. "Lynn was just talking about those talent shows we had." Lemon laughed.

"Yeah," replied Chub. "They were big. Your dad built that stage in your backyard. Man, everyone showed up. Usually right before school started back up."

"He must have done it to keep us close, from running around." Lemon nodded, agreeing with himself. "Lots of singing and dancing, my sisters, Lynn… they were good. People got their turn, lasted all night."

"It was big, no doubt," Chub agreed.

After laughing about some of the neighborhood characters, there was a brief lull. Lemon then stared at Steve McCray and said, "You think we should tell him?" Chub gave him an unsure expression. "You know, what we saw!" Lemon became animated.

"Oh, yeah. Hey, telling him everything else." Chub looked back at Lemon.

I was wondering what it was, but it seemed pretty substantial. Maybe worth writing about. Lemon got it going. He said Chub and him were standing out back of his house one summer night, just bullshitting. It was dark, but not real late. They both saw it. A big something in the sky moving slowly, almost even with the skyline. Larger than a blimp, it had a dome top and a ring of lights around it. For maybe 10 seconds, it hovered, mesmerizing and silencing the two 13-year-olds. Then it was gone, almost like it never happened.

"Stephen, I'm telling you, it was real!" Chub backed him up. "We both saw it, just couldn't comprehend it. We were scared and excited."

"We didn't know what to do!" Lemon offered. "We were frozen for a while, man, then it was like what do we do with that?"

Chub nodded. "Yeah wanted to run and tell somebody, but we thought no one would believe us."

"Then they'd just make fun of us for the rest of the summer and call us crazy," Lemon said.

So, the two Beltzhoover boys kept it only between them for over 50 years, until that moment. They almost seemed relieved, yet surprised, that the secret finally came out.

We talked a couple more minutes, then went inside to say goodbye to Mrs. McCray and Lynn. I asked if I could return and get some thoughts from them. Carrie McCray said I was welcome anytime. I knew I would be back.

Lemon had an agenda, did he ever. We were now headed to Penn Hills, to visit his first true love, Sharon Johnson. He talked her up for the entire 15-minute drive. She obtained a master's in psychology from Duquesne, was an outstanding, serious student, and, on top of that, beautiful.

"You'll see, Stephen, I'm not lying!"

I believed him, then asked, "How did you land her?" Lemon laughed. "She'll tell you, my brother."

Sharon unlocked three deadbolts and let us in. Even wearing a mask, she lived up to the billing.

Relatively tall and slender, it was apparent she was a beauty. She led us to her living room, which looked like no one lived there. A nice home in a middle-class neighborhood, it had been Sharon's home for life.

Sharon, mild-mannered and soft-spoken, had a delightful personality. You could see how Lemon could have been taken in as a young man. It was also evident that they were still good friends who respected each other. For some reason, Lemon sat on the floor while we talked, having a good angle on both Sharon and me.

Sharon, a graduate of Sacred Heart High School and then Duquesne University, never left home. She earned a master's degree in psychology and, for years, worked as a director in youth social services in the city. She has a younger sister, Karen, and when their father passed away, Sharon, the oldest daughter, helped her mom, sister, and grandparents get by. She shared her family's deeply held religious views, which she demonstrated. I noticed in the background that soft gospel music played while we talked. Everything about the house, and Sharon in particular, exuded calm.

She met Lemon at Kennywood after recently completing eighth grade. Lemon had just finished sixth grade but had the mature looks and build of a boy two or three years older. Sharon admitted she was smitten but said her strict parents didn't allow her to talk with boys. Despite that and the fact that they attended different schools, the two developed a close relationship over the next two years. Although Sharon's parents initially liked Lemon, after a while they became suspicious that there was some 'hanky panky' going on, and they forced them to break up. Lemon, completely infatuated with Sharon, was now forbidden to come to the house. He was devastated, and little did he know at the time that there would be more bad news soon to follow.

After Lemon's two-year forced exile, he returned to Pittsburgh and South Hills High School as a junior. At the same time, Sharon Johnson, the serious honors student, was beginning her freshman year at Duquesne. They continued as friends, seeing each other only occasionally during the school year. Lemon was busy with sports while Sharon was working toward the Dean's List. During the summer, Sharon worked at a skating rink just minutes from her home. Lemon would catch the bus and hang out while she worked. Sharon relayed that an older boy, a thug, started to spend time at the rink. He took a liking to the attractive Duquesne co-ed and, as she put it, "got fresh." The bad boy kept coming around, making Sharon extremely nervous. She mentioned it to Lemon, who didn't like it one bit. He showed up the next night. Sure enough, the older thug was at it again, trying to make a move on her. This time Lemon was quickly upon him, and after a quick exchange of words, the fists began to fly. The brawl spilled outside and, surprisingly, was short-lived. Lemon, with his quick explosiveness, had taken care of the older boy in short order. Sharon, averse to violence, hated to see the blood, but at the same time loved the fact that Lemon proved to be her savior.

While Lemon remained madly in love with Sharon, it was her younger sister by three years, Karen, that Lemon actually hung out with. Often, when Sharon turned in early after a day of being responsible, she gladly allowed Karen to be the one to further entertain the action hunter, Lemon. Karen, herself a star student, was more outgoing and funnier than her older sister. She and Lemon would ride around and find action and parties to go to. Attractive like Sharon, Karen possessed a much wilder side. Strictly as friends, Lemon and Karen became traveling partners.

Due to that different relationship, I felt it was important to get Karen's take on Lemon during those late teen years. Sharon gave her sister a call, and for the next 20 minutes, it was Karen Johnson's show. For years of living outside DC in suburban Virginia, Karen was nearing retirement as the head of human resources at a major government office. She backed up Lemon's view that they were friends in mischief as high schoolers, while Sharon was always the adult. Karen described Lemon and her as 'night owls'. When told how well Lemon had fit in at Bedford in those two years, Karen wasn't the least surprised. She always felt that Lemon's greatest asset was his ability to fit in, no matter the environment. She called him a chameleon. Once she said that, I had to agree. Thinking about it, Lemon's greatest ability was simply being Lemon. No one else could do it. His natural friendliness, his warmth, and his constant search for fun and the best in others were wildly contagious.

After speaking with Karen, we soon began to leave. I thanked Sharon for her time and gave her the Covid fist bump. She and Lemon hugged on the way out; their now different kind of love quite evident. Going to the car, Lemon shook his head and said, "Man, Stephen!" I think I knew. Sharon was the keeper he could never keep.

Sharon's interview put an end to the day's work. The next day, we'd spend exclusively in Beltzhoover. Now we drove back to the house with a big meal waiting for us that my wife Jackie had prepared. Also waiting were my son Lance, his wife Kristina, and the boys Miles, six, and Charlie, three, at the time. They had come to eat also but mainly were there to meet Lemon.

As Lemon pulled into the driveway, Miles sprinted out of the house. He seemed excited to see Lemon, but Lance told me later that it was more that Papa had a real friend that had Miles fired up.

As soon as Lemon crawled out of the car, Miles was talking to him. He even ran inside to give Lemon a bottle of water. Lemon turned to me and said, "Man, Miles is something else!"

After eating, we all went to the deck out back and visited. There was an easy rapport between Lemon, Lance, and Kristina. Jackie, as usual, prevented any lulls in the conversation. Soon Miles was dribbling around and shooting at the adjustable hoop we got him for his birthday a couple of weeks earlier. Lemon fed Miles for at least 10 minutes before Miles started to take him to the hole. Lemon laughed. "He's going to be you, Stephen!"

Now that it was time to go home, Charlie was warming up to Lemon. Both Miles and Charlie said goodbye, then ran to Lemon and gave him a hug. Lemon smiled that big smile, while the sight in front of me made me feel good.

The next morning, we hit Beltzhoover around 9:30. We drove up to one of the highest points in the already elevated Beltzhoover. Lemon had never talked much about George before today. Lemon quickly hopped out of the car, and as I stepped out onto the street, he told me to wait a minute while he ran inside. I stood around and surveyed the neighborhood and quickly noticed what a steep drop it was from the side of Georgia's house to the bottom of the hill. A stumble or a push in the back could easily land you in the hospital or a funeral home. I was up high in the South Hills, no doubt. I waited for at least 10 minutes, wondering what the heck was going on in there. As I leaned up against Lemon's car with my interview notebook in hand, I wondered if George might be having second thoughts about speaking with me. After all, he didn't know me, and just because Lemon knew me might not be enough for him to share any thoughts. Plus, I was a lone white man in a black community.

Lemon popped his head out of the front door and gave me a big wave to come inside. As I walked to the front door, I ran into George's wife, Barbara, who looked to be heading out for the day. She was fixed up and gave me a warm smile after Lemon introduced us. At the same time, George appeared at the front door in a bathrobe and slippers. George also gave me a warm smile, extended his hand to me, and welcomed me inside. George led us through a small living room into his kitchen. He appeared to be about the same height as me, so I thought at the very least we had that in common. I noticed he walked with a pronounced limp. Lemon and I sat down at the kitchen table while George offered me coffee, which I declined, then asked me if I wanted a bottle of water. I accepted, and he reached into the fridge and got one for all of us. Some 70s music was playing in the background, and I mentioned that's what I preferred myself. "Marvin Gaye? Come on, man, they don't make that anymore," George said. I had to agree while Marvin sang the musical question, What's Going On?

We discussed quite a bit about sports during the next hour or so. George was a star running back at South Hills High School and, in fact, scored the winning touchdown his senior year to win the city championship. At 6'0" 190, he mixed speed and power to his advantage. So impressive were his exploits that Kentucky State had offered him a full ride to play football. His success didn't end in the fall. George Bradford was also a stellar performer in track. He won a silver medal at the PIAA state meet, narrowly missing the gold. Later, George would say his wife, Barbara, was his gold. *Smooth line*, I thought. Bet he pulled that one out from time to time. Some years after graduation, George was honored for his athletic achievements by being inducted into the South Hills Sports Hall of Fame. Apparently, in anticipation of the interview, George had his plaque and clippings at the ready to show me in case I had any doubts. He was saying, "Don't think Lemon's the only star around!"

Just as he was beginning summer camp at Kentucky State, he discovered his girlfriend was pregnant. A no-brainer for George, he quickly made it home to Pittsburgh and Barbara. 50 years, five children, and 20 grandchildren later, George and Barbara have remained a constant in the ever-changing Beltzhoover.

With impending fatherhood, George felt his best option was the military, even though in 1969 Vietnam was in full swing. Never one to shy away from a challenge, George enlisted in the Marines. Like many young men of color and whites with little means, he fought the wealthy and politicians' war. There would be no senator's son next to him in the jungle. George in Nam for over a year for over a year, and whether it was luck, the grace of God, or his raw athletic ability, young Mr. Bradford returned home unscathed.

The limp had nothing to do with Nam. A serious car accident had resulted in a limp for life. No more leaping over hurdles for the former star, at least not the track kind.

On the trip over to visit George, Lemon had mentioned that in high school, no one messed with the powerful running back. "I'm telling you, Stephen," Lemon said. "He was bad; he could fight!" Apparently, anyone with any sense knew you didn't screw with George Bradford. But as we all know, there will always be a few people who don't get the memo. Those were the ones who could quickly find themselves on the ground with the fists of fury from George.

Long past his days of athletic glory and fighting a war abroad and at home, George began to immerse his energy to church and the Lord. It made all the sense in the world to him. He wanted to be more solid for his family, for everyone. In 1995, he became a lay minister at a Pittsburgh church. It was about the same time as The Million Man March in DC. George led two buses full of congregants to the march for justice and spirituality. He said it further invigorated and motivated him to be a leader in the church. George remains committed to his church today.

Perhaps of all the stories that George shared, it was the following which struck me the most.

Recently returned from the Marines, George returned to the South Hills High track to watch Lemon compete. It was the Spring of 74, and Lemon was the top hurdler in the city. Anticipating his kid brother blowing away the competition, George watched intently as Lemon, with his explosive speed and smooth form, took a huge lead. On the last hurdle, Lemon caught it and went sprawling on the track. Within seconds, he had gone from first to last. George remembered jumping up and yelling the most important thing he could – "Get Up!" Lemon did and ran across the finish line. George said it made him so proud.

I mentioned that getting up is great advice for all of us. We all take our spills.

George smiled. "It sure is my brother. You've got to get up and move ahead."

Further down the hill, on one of the main drags of Beltzhoover, set the house of Gloria and her sister Joyce. Gloria, a childhood friend of the Bradfords, had just returned from the hairdresser and was sporting a smart doo.

As Lemon and I settled in on the screened-in porch with Gloria and Joyce, a car quickly pulled up and stopped in front of the house. Leaving the car in the middle of the street, out jumped an athletic-looking, 60s-something man with a cigarette hanging from his lips.

"Bobby!" Lemon yelled. "Man, what're you doing?"

Bobby Alsberry, Lemon's childhood neighbor and track teammate at South Hills High, walked over to Lemon, and they shared a shake and hug. Lemon introduced us.

"Well, you know, mainly taking care of Dad now. He's 95 and has Alzheimer's." Bobby blew out some smoke and shrugged. Lemon nodded.

Bobby explained that he lived four houses down from the Bradfords back in the day. He said he often showed up near dinner time and stayed and ate. "Man, those girls could cook!" Alsberry also talked about running the third leg of the 440 relay with Lemon, who was the anchor. "Just had to keep it right there, man. Lemon would bring it home for us."

A little smaller talk then Bobby was off, heading back to his dad.

When the conversation resumed on the porch, it quickly became evident that Gloria had a lot of grievances. Gloria did most of the talking, while Joyce would chime in on big points of emphasis.

Their father was biracial and was a custodian at the Catholic Church, while their mother worked at the downtown post office. Gloria claimed that her dad 'never saw color' in his dealings with others. Their family was the second black family to move into their immediate neighborhood.

"Back then," she said, "there were more whites than blacks in Beltzhoover."

Gloria, like Chub McCray, spoke of the bustling community Beltzhoover was in when growing up. She also pointed to the trust of the people and how close knit the community was then.

"Back doors were always open," Gloria said with a look of amazement. "Can you imagine?"

"Yeah," Joyce agreed. "But not now!"

When I asked what caused the change in Beltzhoover, Gloria quickly pointed to the construction of the Civic Arena. An enclosed architectural wonder in the mid-60s, it would be home to the Pittsburgh Penguins, Pitt Basketball, concerts, and other entertainment. However, to build the massive structure, it would require more space than was available. The city's solution was to tear down the lower Hill District, with its heavy population of blacks, to make room. Since most of the homes in the Hill District weren't appraised even at a modest level, eminent domain payments did the residents little good. They were forced to move to the Upper Hill or to communities such as Beltzhoover to start over. Due to Beltzhoover's thriving economy, it lured many of The Hill to relocate there. However, with an economic downturn on the horizon and the slowing down of the steel mills, which eventually closed, the ripple effect was enormous. With the influx of blacks and the economy on a downswing, whites began to leave. 'White flight' was in full force.

With people out of work and youth with little to do, the streets of Beltzhoover were suddenly not so safe. With the increase in crime and violence, Gloria and Joyce both feel nervous.

"When the streetlights go on, we go inside and lock the door," Gloria said. Young people seemed angry. With little prospects, then throwing Covid into the mix, Gloria said things were tough.

According to Gloria, the city was rezoned, and Beltzhoover would no longer have businesses to start. The recent rumor that Beltzhoover could be wiped off its name and annexed to Mt. Washington was another major concern.

The potential of gentrification and higher taxes has instilled a real fear and anger within Gloria that they could end up losing their home.

Gloria has grievances. As well, she should.

After a quick lunch at a Jamaican joint in neighboring Allentown, we returned to the middle of Beltzhoover to visit Janice Tyler. When Lemon was a kid in the streets of Beltzhoover, Janice was a young woman raising kids. Lemon proclaimed her to be one of the real I lookers in the neighborhood – a stone-cold fox, if you will. Although only 13 when Lemon was born, Janice considered Lemon her own. Along with her mother, the well-known and respected 'Mama Tig', they and other women were central figures in the raising of the motherless Lemon.

Lemon slowly rolled his car to a stop in front of Janice's house. She was waiting on the porch of her modest, yet well-kept house. Once Lemon emerged from the car, Janice rose from her chair and yelled, "Jimmy Lemon!" She placed her hands together as if in prayer and beamed at the man she once called her first son. Standing, Janice was above average height and, although nearly 80, still had to be considered a fine-looking woman. Lemon was right. She met Lemon at the steps of the porch and gave him a tight hug. She then shook my hand.

Aware that I was coming, Janice appeared relaxed and friendly. As we sat, she got up, went inside, and returned with two cans of Genesee beer and a bag of pretzels. It was interviewing time.

"Jimmy," Janice said, was a quiet, smart, and curious youngster. Also, so loveable!

I glanced at Lemon, who had a big grin on his face, and asked, "What happened?" He laughed and shrugged his shoulders.

I asked where the name Jimmy Lemon came from. Neither Lemon nor Janice seemed to know or even care. It just was. Very similarly, when I asked Lemon's siblings about the origin of his nickname, they all had different versions. Later, when I brought that to his attention, he seemed unfazed.

Janice for many years taught Sunday School and she said how much Lemon loved to attend. I looked at Lemon and said, "Again, what happened?"

As she spoke more of her personal life, it was apparent Janice Tyler was a woman who knew how to get things done. In addition to raising four children, Janice had been a railroad dispatcher at Station Square, and in the 70s and 80s worked the rails in McKees Rocks, entering car numbers into the computer system. As a volunteer, Janice worked closely with seniors in the area and helped initiate the Beltzhoover Community Parades. She also wrote grants to bring money into Beltzhoover for various activities.

Speaking of the community, Janice echoed what others had said, that 50 or 60 years ago, Beltzhoover was tight-knit and self-contained. She felt the backslide began in the 70s when steel mills slowed and the city started tearing down the projects, which forced people into Beltzhoover, dramatically altering the landscape.

The only mention she made of Lemon's father, Mr. Bradford, was that he was the first black harness racer from the Pittsburgh area. I had the sense that it gave him a certain amount of status in the community. Lemon had never mentioned that fact.

Lemon looked at Ms. Tyler while tilting his head to the side and softly said, "I still feel bad about Eddie; I miss him."

Janice's eyes quickly watered. "Well, you know, it's every day with me, Jimmy."

She turned to me. "Did you know about my Eddie?"

Before I could respond, Lemon told her he hadn't filled me in.

"Hold on, dears." Janice smoothly got up and went into her house.

Lemon, in a low voice, quickly brought me up to speed. "Eddie died some years back – cancer."

"He was a great boxer, went pro."

Janice came out of the house with an arm full of pictures. "Here's some pictures of Eddie and my other kids." One photo showed a young Janice with her kids. Probably no older than mid-twenties, Lemon's assessment was correct – Janice Tyler had been a serious looker.

"Damn, Janice, you were hot!" Lemon practically yelled. She laughed at that, then handed me a picture of Eddie 'The Iceman' Tyler. With his boxing gloves and trunks on, he was staring intensely at the camera. The Iceman, Lemon said, was a top-ranked middleweight in the Pittsburgh area. After turning professional, Eddie, for a short while, was considered somewhat of a contender.

On several occasions, Eddie took the ring at Madison Square Garden, where he was one of Donald Trump's fighters. Immediately, I had to wonder if he ever got paid. Janice relayed that she once traveled to the Big Apple to take in one of Eddie's fights. She said Mr. Trump couldn't have been nicer. "Anything you want," Donald told her. After a slight pause, she turned to me and wondered, "What happened to that man?" Lemon and I both broke out into laughter.

The last item she showed us was a giant blanket, which showed The Iceman in his boxing pose with that intense stare. "He gave this to me on Mother's Day. Have kept it close always, Jimmy."

"It's beautiful, Janice, beautiful," Jimmy softly said. I had to agree.

We left Janice and Beltzhoover for the final visit of the day in Green Tree. His sister Helen, slightly younger than Mable, has a nice apartment with her husband Robbie, on the hill just minutes from the Eat'n Park where we had met Malcolm. The back patio overlooked the parkway, west to the airport, and east into the city.

Helen's looks were strikingly similar to Mable's. Although taller, her facial features, and even more so, her voice, were very close. She was dressed to go out, it appeared, and early on I felt a calm, poised vibe flowing from her.

The only odd thing upon entering Helen's was the sight of Malcolm sitting upright on her living room sofa. What was he doing here? I quickly thought, *Man, can't take anymore Q.* Lemon greeted Helen and his brother and didn't seem surprised or annoyed by seeing Malcolm. I had to wonder if Lemon had jumped Malcom about his weak interview, and this was some make-up time.

Although Helen was extremely friendly and welcoming to me, she was in the midst of fixing a big roast beef dinner, the smell of which was driving me crazy. Lunch at the Jamaican place seemed so long ago. Soon Robbie came in from work and sat on the couch, not far from Malcolm. He was wearing a t-shirt and had the look of a man who had done some real work. He gave me a nod, but also a quick glance of uncertainty. While I declined a couple of offers of water and cranberry juice from Helen, Robbie spoke up and said, "Maybe the man wants a Pepsi." I said yes to that, Robbie nodded, got up, and grabbed one for both of us. I felt totally in at that point.

Soon Helen, moving smoothly and efficiently, had the entire dinner on the table, forcing Robbie from the sofa to his chair at the table. While they began to eat, she mentioned that after dinner they would be going to their Wednesday evening church meeting, where she served as secretary. Helen, a graduate of Duquesne University, and a retired veteran of city social work, gave me the impression she was a woman used to getting things done.

Looking around, I noticed Lemon had left the room, and while Helen and Robbie were engaged in eating, it left the serious-looking Malcolm staring at me. Without any warning, Malcolm began to hold court. The Bradfords' older half-brother, he began to recount his years growing up on The Hill. Raised primarily by his grandmother Ruth, who ran numbers and for a living since his mother was still a child herself, 14 when Malcolm arrived. Terribly young, but not as young as when his older brother Henry was born and their mother Vera was only 12.

Apparently, the father in both cases was a serviceman during WWII. I suppose statutory rape must not have been viewed as seriously in the 40s, especially if you were a black girl.

Malcom discussed his role in his grandmother's numbers racket. It was in Malcolm's bedroom, under the wooden floor slats, that Grandma Ruth hid the betting slips. Later in the day, Malcolm would deliver those slips to a nearby "businessman".

According to Malcom, everything you needed was on The Hill. Like Beltzhoover, it was a self-contained community. He stressed that he always, even as a kid, had his own money. Malcolm delivered newspapers and fish from the wagon he pulled behind him. The fish he would sell to markets, most of which were run by Jews.

After finishing their meal, Helen and Robbie quietly left for church while Malcom continued with his almost documentary-like tales of The Hill District. Unlike Lemon, Malcolm Williams was not prone to an expressive nature with his face or voice.

Further detailing the autonomous nature of The Hill in the 50s and 60s, he said there were three movie shows within five blocks. Also, there were plenty of shops and stores to frequent. There was also an infamous, mean black detective named Mason, who patrolled the area and ruled with an iron fist. Malcolm figured the Pittsburgh Police believed a black officer would be better accepted in their neighborhood. But Mason was both feared and hated within the community. As a kid, he witnessed Mason shoot a guy in an alley that had robbed Schwartz's Fish Market. "It blew my mind," a stone-faced Malcom said. "He was one cold man, I tell you."

Malcolm mentioned that back in the day, Italians didn't mind associating with blacks. Maybe because they were 'the niggers' not too many years before. During the summer, he would swim with some of his Italian friends a couple of days a week. His grandmother, at one point, was even married to an Italian man. Malcolm, at an early age, was exposed to all kinds of action and diversity on The Hill.

It was through Malcolm's 'documentary' that I first learned of the coming together of Arthur and Vera Bradford. Arthur, 'Mr. Bradford', was a regular at Grandma Ruth's house of numbers. Vera, not believed to be an employee of her mother's, was very visible, especially to Mr. Bradford's eyes. He was taken by Vera's beauty to the point of obsession. He had to have her! Although only 16, with two boys, Malcolm one of them, Arthur Bradford made a proposal to Ruth to take away her daughter. The deal was this – Mr. Bradford, 36, would help Ruth buy a new home if she agreed to let Vera live with him. The deal was struck, and the Bradford family's incredible, tumultuous story was off and running.

Malcolm more than made-up for his showing at Eat n Park just two days earlier. He had painted a clear picture of himself and life on The Hill, which I had little knowledge of. Interestingly, Lemon was in an adjoining room throughout the entire interview. It was a good strategic move on his part. The two of them together apparently weren't conducive to a good interview.

On the way to the car, Malcolm paused and couldn't help himself. "Remember, August, Elvis, and Michael Jackson return." Lemon, just moments before so pleased with his big brother's rebound, now shook his head in disgust. "I'm waiting on some new tunes, then," was my reply. We drove back to my house. The day was done.

I called Helen a few days later since my trip to Green Tree had turned into a visit with Malcom. I asked her to share what she felt was important for me to best understand Lemon, the Bradfords, and Beltzhoover.

On the phone, she came across the same as she was in person: poised, calm, well-spoken, and friendly. Helen talked about how Beltzhoover and the chaos of the Bradfords motivated her to use education as an escape route. A self-described bookworm, Helen was more serious and disciplined than her siblings. Always a good student, she pushed herself to become even better. While the neighborhood would buzz with activity during the evenings, Helen would close her door and devote her time to homework and reading.

Upon graduation from South Hills High School, she enrolled at Duquesne University. During her freshman year, she quickly discovered about white attitudes and expectations. A professor on the first day of class questioned why she was there, that she had little chance of passing his course. Helen proved the educated bigot wrong, pulling a 'B' and beginning her journey as a Sociology major and graduate. Helen was the lone college graduate of the family and was determined to put her degree to work. She worked for years in the city, serving youth and families. With four children of her own, Helen laughed that she put her sociology degree to work just as much at home!

She turned her conversation to high school days in the 60s when South Hills High School had more whites than blacks. Due to this, they were considered a 'White' city school, which gave them an invitation to Kennywood Park for class trips and picnics. 'Black' city schools like Fifth Avenue, Schenley, and Carrick went to West View Park for their fun.

Before the civil rights movement and legislation, the Kennywood pool was reserved for whites only. When the law forced Kennywood to open their pool to all or close, they chose to shut it down. No blacks on that pure Kennywood water seemed to be the message. Helen provided me with a piece of Pittsburgh history I was unaware of. I was learning from these interviews.

Helen's take on Lemon was that he was still searching, trying to find his identity, and how his life turned out the way it did. She empathized with his hurt and confusion over being abandoned by his mother at 18 months, but his pain was delayed. Helen,8, and Mable, 10, when Vera left, along with the others, felt the panic and sting immediately. Growing up, Lemon wanted more from his siblings, but they were all traveling their own difficult path forward. Amazingly, in their own ways, they all found their way out. Helen did it with her books and strength.

I must believe she was a great social worker.

I had met with many of Lemon's beginnings in Beltzhoover. All the ones he felt were crucial to my understanding of him. I was done with his well-thought-out schedule of interviews. However, when I left the McCray's that day, the last words of Ms. McCray stayed with me. "You need to come back soon."

Carrie McCray was right. I did need to come back to Beltzhoover and her house one more time. From Lemon's descriptions of her being so watchful of him and other neighborhood kids and Chub's story of his mom's giving 'the wave' to kids who couldn't pay in the cafeteria lunch line, I knew she was a person I had to talk to.

Lemon, as a youngster, complained that Carrie McCray was always on his ass. Yet when older, realized she cared and was trying to make up for the absence of Vera Bradford.

Speaking with Ms. McCray on the back deck, as I had with her son Steve, it was evident that she was a woman who always had a finger on the pulse of her community. She first became familiar with Beltzhoover by being a March of Dimes volunteer. Going door to door and gathering donations, she was able to get to know her neighbors. Carrie, still sharp and alert at 91, had been a nursing student until her daughter became ill, and she was forced to drop out. Her husband, Leon, was the primary breadwinner as an employee at the U.S. Post Office. While raising her children, Ms. McCray continued to work. Having passed a civil service test, she became an examiner with the employment agency. Eventually, she was hired as a cafeteria worker at South Hills High School. She enjoyed contact with the students, but it also allowed her a closer look at the high school and her own children.

Before the advent of free and reduced lunches, Ms. McCray was known for the 'Big Wave' through the lunch line, for the kids that needed it. She was keenly aware of those students and, to this day, took pride in her actions.

Heavily involved in her children's education, she helped lead the effort to eliminate corporal punishment in the district schools. Carrie also fought to keep Beltzhoover youth in their neighborhood elementary and junior high schools instead of being bused 40 minutes outside the city.

She viewed it as taking young kids out of their comfort zone into an area of more pressure and unease.

In a life of service, perhaps her greatest accomplishment and source of pride, related to her 12 years as a church youth group leader of integrated students. Young teens, black and white, from the city and suburbs, would receive an education not only on the Good Word but also on the real world of current events. Carrie explained she wanted her kids to be aware of the world around them and how people were affected by life. Her goal was to foster openness and care to their minds for solutions.

Ms. McCray's eyes lit up when she described how past students, now in their 50s and 60s, continue to write and call her to keep in touch and, at times, seek her counsel. What a tribute, I told her. It shows the impact she had in their lives and how they still loved her. She smiled slightly and became teary-eyed. Carrie went on to talk about her classes. She encouraged open discussion and debate. Her main rule was to not interrupt. She felt too many leaders today do not follow the advice she gave her youth group students.

When it came to Lemon, it was apparent Ms. McCray viewed him as one of her own. It was apparent to Lemon as well; even though he at times resented her discipline, Lemon always makes a point to visit her whenever he is in town. She remembered Lemon as a very sweet, open child, who hung out with her son growing up. They were very active, but she felt he usually avoided any big trouble. She loves Lemon.

When you love someone, your voice goes soft, your face relaxes, but your eyes come alive, rejoicing in remembrance. The loved one can be gone for years, but that feeling is unchanged, unchained from your being. A connection that cuts through pain, struggling, and hardships and holds close the wonder and joy of life.

Such was the reaction and countenance of Carrie McCray when I asked about her late husband, Leon. He had passed away four years earlier, at the age of 89.

Leon McCray had a 35-year career with the U.S. Post Office, where he eventually became the manager at the Bloomfield office. In order to help support their family of seven children, Leon often worked additional jobs, like taxicab driver – If that wasn't enough, Leon began mid-life studies at the University of Pittsburgh and earned his bachelor's degree in English in 1971. Whenever Lynn and Steve would complain about the rigor of their college studies, their father felt little sympathy. After retiring from the postal service, Leon put his degree to work by substitute teaching in the Pittsburgh Public School system and then working for the Department of Environmental Resources. Leon McCray was one accomplished human being.

Through all of his achievements, it was his role as an elder in the Grace Memorial Presbyterian Church in the Upper Hill District which was the most impactful and long-lasting contribution to the city of Pittsburgh.

In the late 1960s, during one of the country's and Pittsburgh's biggest periods of racial strife, church leaders were to vote on whether to merge with the longtime white congregation of Bellefield Presbyterian Church in Oakland. Advocates viewed it as a chance to show how races could come together to worship. Others were not feeling so hopeful and strongly resisted the idea. For Leon, the choice was clear. He cast the deciding vote to join churches.

Ms. McCray said she and her husband wanted their children to have a broad knowledge of different kinds of people. Fifty years later, the ecumenical church that Leon McCray helped create still thrives. Now known as the Community of Reconciliation, it is affiliated with the Presbyterian, Methodist, United Church of Christ, and Christian churches. The congregation is a 50/50 split of blacks and whites, a rarity in such a divided country as ours.

The McCrays' lives and actions demonstrated their commitment to not only their family but the entire community around them. Living just across the street from the chaotic Bradfords, they showed how different people can unite, share, and grow together.

I have known Mable Bradford Washington for over 50 years, as Lemon's older sister, the wife of my first Bedford sports idol, Gary 'Goo' Washington, and as the co-founder and driving force behind Extended Family, a much-needed alternative school in Bedford County.

It was her husband, Goo, who was my first exposure to a black person. It was a very positive and impactful exposure, which I'm sure helped pave the way to my openness toward people of color.

I was a young elementary school kid when Goo was the star power-hitting first baseman of my father, John Waltman's Bedford High School baseball team. A left-handed hitter, Goo was known for his prodigious blasts to deep right into and sometimes over a thicket of high grass and weeds. Dad, a former professional pitcher, regretfully had witnessed first-hand a number of long home runs in his career. My father, with this experience, estimated some of

Goo's long drives to be over 400 feet. Unbelievable for a kid still in high school!

Not only a standout on the baseball diamond, but Goo Washington was also an outstanding lineman on the football team. With his quickness and power, Goo, from his pulling guard position, would pave the way for a devastating Bison running game. He was also the stopper on Bedford's defensive line. Long-time Bedford football fans still recount the incredible come-from-behind touchdown-saving tackle he made at Claysburg. Witherspoon, one of the fastest and best running backs in the Altoona area, had broken free into the open for what looked like a sure touchdown. Washington, coming from the defensive line and giving up at least 10 yards, got on his horse and, with an amazing burst of speed, tracked down the speedy Claysburg back before he could score. It amazed and stunned the crowd on both sides of the field.

You must wonder that in a different decade, with his speed and power, Goo might have been a star running back. As it was, Goo earned a football scholarship to Salem College in West Virginia, where he became a three-time all-conference guard. Although he had great success on the gridiron, Goo loved to play baseball. In fact, the baseball coach at Salem, aware of his power stroke, recruited him for the baseball team. Goo wanted to play, but his football coach wouldn't allow it.

As an 8-year-old, Goo's mighty blasts made quite an impact on me. Dad, at the supper table, sometimes would say, "That damn Goo, my God, what power!" But it was at a high school dance, that surprisingly my parents chaperoned that Goo made his biggest and everlasting impression on me. Goo, always outgoing and friendly, spotted me and my brother Jeffery in the corner of the gym. Apparently, Mom and Dad didn't want to pay a babysitter, so we were there. He came and started chatting us up. Man, I was thrilled. He even showed us some dance moves and encouraged us to go out on the floor. No one else on the team took the time to do that, and I have always remembered it. Having a sports hero pay attention to you sticks in your memory.

When Goo returned to Bedford, he became a long-time assistant coach in both football and track. Although a tremendous athlete and competitor, Coach Washington impressed me with his empathy toward his players. Capable of lighting a fire under some asses with his booming voice, Goo was more often seen supporting, consoling, and encouraging his athletes. He understood them and cared about them like only a former competitor could.

Over the years, my former idol turned into a good friend. He had served as his brother-in-law Lemon's overseer and protector for two years, and when I was Bedford's basketball coach, he sat in the front row of bleachers directly across from me every game. Goo would stare at me with that intense game face, seemingly saying, "Do you have them ready? Let's get after it!" I loved to see that look moments before tip-off. It fired me up.

Goo, along with his uncle Floyd Harris, have to be the most gifted athletes never to be inducted into the Bedford County Sports Hall of Fame. In his day, Floyd was a great running back at Bedford and track performer. In college, Mr. Harris even ran in the nationally prestigious Penn Relays.

With Goo Washington, not being in the Hall of Fame is not a major concern. He knows who he is and what he has accomplished. Outside of sports, Mr. Washington was also a major contributor to education in Bedford County. Along with Mable, he formed and successfully ran Extended Family, an alternative school serving the county, for over 30 years. Goo and Mable also raised four successful and athletic children. All are college graduates and accomplished.

That's Gary 'Goo' Washington, one impressive human. Now, just wait until you get a load of Mable Bradford Washington!

I met with Mable and Goo in their home on the outskirts of Bedford. Lemon was with me.

Lemon's relationship with his older sister is not unlike many siblings with a large gap in age. Although Mable has always been there for him, he at times gets frustrated with her 'older sister ways'. Mable keeps a close eye on Lemon and isn't hesitant to offer advice or criticism. He, at times, resents it – yet needs it.

Lemon predicted that Mable would be prepared for the interview. She had been asking him numerous questions about the process and even seemed somewhat anxious. But, my God, Lemon, the literary pyromaniac, was on the money. Mable was on!

We sat in the living room; Lemon had sunk into a chair to my left while I was on the couch next to Goo. Mable pulled up a chair from the dining room table and positioned it to be directly across me. Before we started, Goo offered me a Coke, and I accepted. He came back with the can and a glass of ice. His waiting on me I found amusing. "Christ!" I said. "I thought for sure you'd bring me something to eat."

"Huh!" was his response, then laughed.

Mable started off talking hoops. Their grandson Max, a junior, was a starter on the Bedford High School squad, and they were all looking for a strong season. After a few more minutes of basketball talk, Goo turned to me with that 'look', like, "What are you bringing to the party today?"

I explained that they would be a key part of explaining who Lemon was and how he and others in their family came to be. This story would be the follow-up to When Lemon Happened, a prequel which would focus on his youth and life in Beltzhoover. Although Mable was around Lemon in his early years, she was married and out of the house by the time Lemon was 10.

Mable, a youthful 74, still attractive, energetic, and active, possessed those classic Bradford looks – high cheekbones, a strong jawline, and flashing eyes that showed interest. In another life, I thought she'd be an African Queen.

Mable, knowing what I needed, quickly went into some family history, building a foundation for a deeper understanding of not only Lemon but the entire family. She spent a great deal of time talking about her Grandma Ruth, Vera Bradford's mother, who in many ways was the rock of the family. To those who didn't live those years with Mable and her siblings, it might seem odd that a woman who ran numbers could be such a positive force. But what applied to her should apply to all people – it's not your title; it's who you are that counts.

Mable related that Ruth had come from Mississippi and, for years, had been a domestic worker. Eventually, Grandma Ruth became a businesswoman of some success on The Hill. It's all about knowing what the public wants.

Despite the nature of her work, Grandma offered stability to her grandchildren, who were in dire need of it. Ruth, with so many of the Bradford youth around, had to set boundaries and rules for them to follow. She was known to strictly enforce them. To Mable, Ruth was filling the role of both grandmother and mother. Vera, just a child herself, had Henry and Malcolm at the ages of 12 and 14. Much of the burden fell to Ruth.

Ruth was also adamant that all of the children attend church every Sunday, regardless of Saturday night's activities. The kids all obeyed, even when the older ones came crawling in early in the morning.

Mable, like Helen, recounted rare trips downtown to department stores to view the latest styles. Since blacks in the early sixties weren't allowed to try on clothes in the store, they'd have to gamble on the right size because they couldn't return the purchase either. Asked about how that felt, Mable matter of factly responded, "That's the way it was; we knew it." She shrugged her shoulders, but her face and eyes said, "It was screwed up."

Other than exposing them to Jesus, Grandma Ruth taught Mable and her sisters responsibilities such as cooking and cleaning. If you were spending time with Grandma on The Hill, you were working.

After wondering about her oldest half-brother Henry, Mable spent some time filling me in on her late brother's talents. Henry graduated from 5th Avenue High School, where he played basketball and ran track. It was in high school that he started the group The Turbans. Henry was known for having a dynamic baritone voice, and his band played throughout Pittsburgh in black communities, bars, and clubs. Once, Henry convinced his grandmother to allow Mable to sing with his group because they needed a female voice for a few songs. I asked Mable if she had a good voice as well. "I guess," she replied. Goo chimed in and said she has a real good voice. Since Mable was only 13 at the time, Ruth reluctantly let her go, but Henry had to promise he'd take good care of his little sister. He did, and for that night, Mable Bradford, at 13, was fronting the band.

Mable grew up not giving much thought to the carousel of men who frequented her grandmother's home daily. It was normal, just like not being able to try on clothes at Kaufmanns. Like it was normal to take a beating from Mr. Bradford's wooden paddle if she received a grade lower than a 'B'. But for Mable, it was also normal for her to sneak out the bedroom window and make it to a party, praying she didn't get caught. The risk/reward involved was consequential. It was also normal for Mable to help unload lumber from her father's truck with her brothers on Saturdays.

While Mable's normal living wasn't always a good thing, there were moments in the high altitude of Beltzhoover that were quite sublime. For instance, one of the greatest baseball players of all time, Willie Mays, of the San Francisco Giants, would frequent their neighborhood many times to visit relatives who lived across the street. The Say Hey Kid would come out to the streets and talk with the youngsters, give some hitting tips, and sign autographs.

Mays and Roberto Clemente were my favorite players when I was a youngster. Both were talented hitters and outfielders with speed to burn, and who added great excitement to the game. So influential those two stars were on me, I began to use the basket catch in Little League.

As Mable spoke of her past, she seemed to be reliving it. She almost seemed transformed by her own words and memories. Was it just me being caught up in it all, or did her face now appear 30 years younger? I gave a quick glance to Lemon, slumped in his chair to the side. He looked somewhere between mesmerized and puzzled.

She acknowledged that what had been normal as a child had become a burden to carry into adulthood. The adult Mable had the recognition that what had been her life was not so normal. The chaos and violence she grew up with were the polar opposite of her neighbors and friends, the McCray's. Saying life 'was the way it was', routine to them back then, but abnormal and disturbing in the telling of it.

Mable, Goo, and Lemon all agreed that emotions hit you harder after the fact than when you are in the thick of the action. Much like a soldier returning from war, time does not necessarily heal all wounds. Upon reflection, what was buried during the madness in order to survive, would eventually come to the surface and wreak havoc. The Bradfords survived their wars, but not without suffering from their own brand of PTSD.

Surprisingly, Mable seemed to show no animosity toward her mother, Vera, who escaped the harshness of Mr. Bradford but, in doing so, abandoned her children. Perhaps Mable understood, even at a young age, that survival had to be the first order of business.

In the absence of her mother, Mable, the oldest daughter and only 10, was now saddled with cooking and cleaning chores and largely responsible for two younger sisters and two younger brothers. Lemon was 16 months at the time of Vera's exodus. These roles were expected and demanded from Arthur Bradford.

Mable survived her years in Beltzhoover, fulfilling her many roles and also graduating from South Hills High School. Her grades were good enough to avoid regular beatings at the hands of her father. In the Bradford house, that was worth more than making the honor roll.

As was stated earlier, Arthur Bradford was believed to be the first black harness racer in the Pittsburgh area. He often would travel to The Meadows Racetrack to compete, and from time to time, Mable would go to help. It was during one of these trips that she came across a sturdy, strong-built teen named Gary Washington from Bedford. Washington was there with his father, Albert, who not only raced horses but also owned them. That was not a common feat in the 50s and 60s. Albert was known as an accomplished businessman and a man not to be messed with.

It didn't take long for Mable, like Goo, to discover much more passion away from the horses. "What horses?" Goo would say. Away from the track, Mable and Goo started a wild ride of their own, resulting in marriage and their first child at 19. After Goo's college graduation and the end of his football career, they eventually settled in Bedford. Mable, finding the transition challenging to a small, white town, returned to Pittsburgh every other weekend in the early months. She credited the Hamiltons, one of the few black families in town, as a huge help to her. Ellen, in particular, was a friend to turn to, and in fact, they remain close today.

Despite living in Bedford, she received updates on Lemon frequently. While Lemon had always been a friendly, energetic, and active youngster, as he approached early teen years, his recreation began to change. The boys he started to run with had little or no parenting, little money, but loads of anger.

During the late 60s when the Black Panthers rose to prominence, Lemon and his band of brothers were expressing themselves in their own rebellious ways. I looked at Lemon, and he sheepishly said, "Oh yeah, didn't tell you all that."

I asked, "What all did you do?"

Repositioning himself in the chair and sitting up. "Man, Stephen, a lot of shit! We were fools!"

Turning my attention to Lemon, I pressed him on details. He admitted that, at the ages of 13 and 14, he was on the streets quite a bit. Like his friends, he was restless and angry. They fashioned themselves as young Black Panthers. Throwing bottles at passing police cruisers, then sprinting away, and stealing whatever they could get their hands on from empty houses were favorite pastimes of theirs. In one case, they accidentally burned a house down. Screwing around with Molotov cocktails has never been a good thing.

In one tragic case, his one buddy, the wildest and most daring of the group, jokingly tossed a bottle too close to another friend, and it exploded on him. His burns were so horrible that he spent months in the hospital. Lemon felt so much guilt that he visited his friend every week at the hospital. His chaotic, rudderless life was now taking its toll. By the summer of 1970, at the age of 15, it came to a head. Sharon Johnson's forced breakup served only to fuel more anger and an attitude of 'so what?' and 'who cares?'

It was in this environment and state of mind that Lemon agreed to aid his flame-throwing friend to steal a car. He took Mr. Bradford's car to drop off his friend for his city larceny. Escaping through the Liberty Tunnel on the way home, his friend stepped on it a bit too much and rammed the back of Mr. Bradford's vehicle. Scared, they both jumped out of the stolen vehicles and ran like the wind out of the tunnel, heading toward Route 51 and home.

Unfortunately for them, the police were waiting on the other side. The upshot of this resulted in his friend being sent to juvenile detention and Mable receiving a call from Mr. Bradford.

Mable, herself a young wife and mother, was just starting a new life in Bedford. Her father laid out the story and wanted Goo and Mable to attend Lemon's juvenile court hearing in Oakland. Not only that, but Arthur Bradford also said he wanted Mable to take Lemon with her to live in Bedford. Either that, or he was heading to juvenile detention.

Already feeling overwhelmed with her new roles in life and attempting to fit into a small, white town, the thought of being solely responsible for her wild, untamed kid brother seemed too much. She didn't want to do it. Mable admitted that it was Goo who stated she had to. She eventually relented, and despite her fears, called Mr. Bradford back and relayed that they would attend the hearing and offer Lemon a home. Juvenile Detention had to be taken off the table.

As anticipated, the judge granted temporary guardianship to the Washingtons, and Lemon was sentenced to two years in Bedford.

At this point, Lemon chimed in and wondered out loud if he would have been better off if he'd been sent to 'juvie'. "Maybe it would've matured me, made me more responsible. Maybe I would've come out more together."

Goo became animated on the couch, leaned forward, and stomped his foot. "Lemon! You would have come out worse than when you went in!"

"Surrounded by criminals worse than you – you would've fallen into it."

Lemon shrugged. "Maybe."

Those two years in Bedford, at the ages of 15 and 16, were critical to the young man, who had been heading down a dangerous path in the city. Like his older sister, the transition to white, small town Bedford wasn't easy. It was remarkable that during this time, he was a star and largely accepted by his white peers. Most of the credit for his rapid success had to go to Lemon himself. 'The Chameleon' had the keen awareness to quickly size up his new school and town. Once he saw, for the most part, he had been given a clean slate, he relaxed and did what he did best – be himself. Mable and Goo were also largely responsible for his daunting task of assimilation. They knew Bedford, and they knew Lemon. If he heeded their guidance and advice, Lemon had a chance to not only survive but flourish. Goo and Mable also enforced strict discipline. Outside of basketball, track, and school, there would be no running around. No dating, no drinking, no parties allowed. Yes, indeed, the baby brother was on a tight leash.

But in addition to Lemon and the Washingtons, the students at Bedford High School and his teammates had to be recognized for accepting this wondrous city alien and giving him a chance. In time, after initial suspicion and wariness, Lemon realized these white people were alright. No, not all, but the kids he dealt with on a regular basis were good and decent. Lemon had friends, and he had become quite popular. While perhaps older whites in the community weren't completely won over, the youth of this town were.

Mable, unlike any other person I interviewed, not only covered the past but gazed into the future. She felt young people, like her grandson Max, would grow into adulthood unconcerned about color or sexual orientation. I offered that my own son and his friends, now parents themselves, are much more tolerant than our generation. We all agreed that it was slowly moving in the right direction.

We felt that one huge problem with race in this country was that it still in many ways was segregated. Schools, communities, churches, and neighborhoods are often defined and limited by color. The lack of exposure to diversity is stifling to people in small towns like Bedford. For the most part, Bedford's residents are kind, hardworking people who have spent little time with people of color. This lack of real-life experience allows people to fall back on old racial stereotypes to determine their attitudes and beliefs toward them.

A city girl from Pittsburgh, Mable has been a citizen of impact in Bedford for over 50 years. Her resilience and optimism for the future can't be overstated. Like

Beltzhoover's Carrie McCray, Mable Washington belongs to a church that features more than one color. It's an anomaly in a small town like Bedford. The Mt. Pisgah AME Zion Church is a small, white structure that sits on a hill in the west end of town. Known as the 'black church' for years, it now welcomes a substantial number of white members.

To say Mable is a member of the Mt. Pisgah Church would be like saying Lebron James is a member of the Los Angeles Lakers. She is a leader, a go-getter, a woman who makes things happen. No different than many black women in this country, she has always fulfilled the needs of her family and the larger community. It seems to be in the DNA.

To prove the point, here are some of her positions of leadership within the church: Sunday School teacher, church delegate, pastor steward, district Christian Education delegate, missionary team, and church secretary. Also, Mable was once elected to represent the Allegheny Conference at a General Conference in Charlotte, North Carolina. All of this dedication to church and religion was on top of raising four children, directing Extended Family Alternative School, and attending countless football and basketball games. I would like to meet the woman who has given more of herself than she has in the past 50 years.

"People have to get out of their boxes," Mable said. "Boxes with no windows!" boomed Goo.

"I like that!" I smiled. "Maybe just take credit for that line myself."

Mable, her face now looking tired, had given me all she had for well over an hour. "I'm done."

The girl who partly grew up on The Hill, and numbers runner; abandoned by her mother at 10 and forced to take on mother-like responsibilities; who would crawl out of her bedroom window at night, risking a beating, to find a party. That woman was done for the day.

Mable Washington, in essence, is a survivor. A woman who not only survived but made life work well in two vastly different worlds. Her experiences enable her to understand and connect with people from all walks of life. Mable is the best of both worlds.

After leaving the Washington house, Lemon turned to me and said, "Man, Mable was on! I never heard her say those things!"

I agreed; she was on. Mable was like many of her siblings; the interview became a therapy session of sorts. Lemon, along with me, was hearing things for the first time. We were both learning. It had become a common theme with our visits.

It made me wonder about Lemon, though. He shared some of his young teen episodes only after Mable brought it up. While the other Bradfords seemed to be baring their souls, Lemon, after 50 years, still had some secrets.

I hadn't given it much thought, but I should have known that the stolen car incident wasn't his first adventure testing the law. I don't think it matters where you live, but the combination of adolescent energy and boredom, mixed with anger toward absentee parents, will lead to volatility. Although normally good-natured, it's easy to see how he could have easily fallen in with kids living under similar circumstances.

Lemon, who grew up without specific guidelines or expectations that only engaged parents can give, was susceptible to outside influence. He learned early on that his ability to blend in almost anywhere was his ticket to survival. Being an outstanding athlete was also helpful to this end. It's why he was popular not only at South Hills High School but at white Bedford High School as well. He was a gifted chameleon, as his old friend, Karen Johnson had pointed out.

Lemon is now in his late 60s, so the social skills that made him so popular in his youth no longer are as relevant. He wants to be settled, but being unsettled makes it difficult. 'Home' doesn't elicit a clear picture in his mind. His various stops in life have resembled his mind – chaotic, unpredictable, wonderful, and sad. Only his good nature and resilience have kept him from a life of bitterness and extended down days.

As time went on, he could reflect on what he had missed in not having two solid, loving parents in his life. His early years were a muddle of love and confusion, with his siblings, Carrie McCray, Janice Tyler, and Mama Tig, filling the role of his absent mother. It wasn't until he was older that Lemon felt the full impact of a motherless childhood.

What Lemon can now appreciate is that his older siblings had to immediately feel the impact and deal with the consequences of Vera Bradford's departure. They were mere elementary school students at the time. They were alone, facing all of life had to bring in Beltzhoover in the late 50s and 60s. What parenting remained was the harsh discipline of Mr. Bradford. In a sense, the conditions were worse for the older Bradfords.

In a busy life where everyone has their own trials and tribulations, we often don't know the extent of others' challenges and pain. Such was the case for Lemon. He knew his situation wasn't good, and being sent to Bedford for two years was proof of that. But what he couldn't realize was the incredible battles his older brothers and sisters had been engaged in for years. The life stories I heard from them became new awareness and appreciation for Lemon.

In addition to his relationship with his siblings, his more immediate family, daughters Chasitie, 33, and Chazz, 27, are a source of complicated emotions also. Daughters of divorce, Chasitie is a successful production manager at TBS in Atlanta. Intelligent and attractive, she is a source of great pride for Lemon. With Chazz, he sees some of himself. Also, a looker and bright, Chazz is still searching for her place. A mobile young woman, in the past five years, Chazz has lived in Virginia, Texas, Georgia, and now, Los Angeles. A point guard in college, she has produced and starred in quite a few athletic videos on YouTube. Chazz even interviewed Lemon and me on YouTube about my story, when Lemon Happened. She had a hard time keeping it together with our answers and lack of technology skills. We had a great time.

The big hurt for Lemon is that he rarely sees them. The distance between them and his inability to travel on a regular basis makes it difficult to remain close. The girls' hectic lives make it near impossible for them to visit their father on a regular basis as well. That creates a love that hurts.

Lemon's relationships with past girlfriends and wives have never turned into happily-ever-after either. The end of his relationship with Sharon Johnson, his first real love, was difficult for him. The fact that it coincided with his exile to Bedford made it even worse.

Lemon, with his looks and personality, never had trouble landing an attractive girl. However, many years ago, when word reached me that he had married a recent Miss Pennsylvania, I just had to shake my head and smile. That damn Lemon! Who knows exactly why, but this surprising union didn't last a year. Perhaps Lemon's unsettled lifestyle created creeping doubt about her new husband. Maybe the prospects of a comfortable life with Lemon didn't seem likely. For whatever reason, Miss Pennsylvania hit the road.

Lemon's marriage to Chasitie's and Chazz's mother, although lasting much longer, still ended the same. But credit Lemon for never giving up on love. He has had several serious girlfriends since his divorce and was even engaged about six years ago. Unfortunately, all the relationships have met the same fate.

No matter the setbacks, in love or larger life, Lemon remains fully engaged. He has never wanted to quit the game. Once, I asked him if being a star years ago helped him cope with disappointments. Lemon quickly agreed that it did. Although it had been many years ago, he said that feeling of being somebody had never left him. Lemon still carried himself with confidence, with the movements of a winner. The wins might not be plentiful as of late, but like any good athlete, he believes they are coming.

Mable encouraged me to sit in on the next Bradford family Zoom call. They got together every Sunday to catch up and air grievances. I shared with Mable that I was never a big fan of the Zoom call. They were often chaotic, plus I always carried the slight fear that it could quickly turn into an intervention. However, I wasn't passing this one up.

It was January 22, 2023, with the Bengals and Bills soon to do battle. Mable apologized for the meeting falling so close to the big AFC playoff game but felt they should stay consistent. We all jumped on Helen's number, and after Helen welcomed me, the meeting began. In attendance were Helen, Mable, Malcolm, Lemon, and Dottie, the sister I had yet to meet, who lived in Virginia. Ruthie, who was closest to Lemon in age, had passed away the month before, succumbing to cancer.

After some brief discussion of football and what seemed like familiar talk of kids and grandkids, the talk became more pointed. The conversation shifted to their younger years with Mr. Bradford. Dottie, who initiated much of the discussion, brought up how their dad once told her ladies don't whistle. She also recalled that he didn't permit any music in the house before noon. Mable quickly added that if you strayed from the rules, that's when the beatings began.

Malcolm, the elder of the clan, seemed to be granted deference due to his position. He came across as comfortable in his role and filled it well. He quickly pointed out that Mr. Bradford was a product of his times. "Nobody taught him anything!"

Helen felt you can't hold resentment; it only does you harm. Yet, she said he was wrong. The lack of affection and emotional support was damaging.

"You can't blame Daddy forever," Dottie said. Interestingly, it was the first time I had heard Mr. Bradford called daddy.

Mable shot a look, which conveyed that she certainly could blame him forever.

Dottie admitted that in her early days of motherhood, she spanked her kids. "But I never felt good about it." She even attended classes to make better choices to avoid corporal punishment. Dottie never went back to it.

Malcolm threw in that he never spanked his kids, but that they spank their own. Everyone got a kick out of that.

Mable added that she never gave up on spanking. However, if you discipline early, she felt kids didn't need to be hit. The intense, devastating look would do the trick if they knew you were willing to back it up. Goo once admitted to me that Mable's glare could even rattle him.

George entered the Zoom late, most likely due to wrapping up his church service. Seemingly knowing this stage of the conversation, he added that although Arthur Bradford wasn't often available, he did watch him hurdle a couple of times. George said something to the effect that they were all adults now and they still had today.

Lemon, for his part, had little to say. He, the baby, mainly listened to his older brothers and sisters. He did urge me to tell them about the book, which I did. I let them know the writing was nearly completed and that if I could get some pictures from them, I'd include them in the book.

This led to several minutes of questioning about who was in possession of old family pictures. The consensus was that no one did. The siblings agreed there wouldn't be many anyways. Picture-taking wasn't the thing back in the day, especially when there was no camera. Photos growing up were mainly class pictures or related to sports. I asked them to search and give me what they had.

As the Bengals-Bills kickoff was rapidly approaching, George offered a prayer to put a lid on the Bradford Zoom. He delivered eloquent words, thanking the Lord for this time together with family. He praised Him for the gifts he had bestowed upon all of them. George was thankful for today and the days that would follow. Life is precious.

The Bradfords said Amen, and I had to agree.

Epilogue

With improved health, Lemon has returned to his home city of Pittsburgh. He has an apartment ten minutes from his old neighborhood of Beltzhoover, and fifteen minutes from me. We recently had lunch and talked about seeing some high school basketball games. We laughed quite a bit. He was at his best – which is, being Lemon.